Stringpops

GW00459238

James Bond

Three pieces for flexible string ensemble
with piano accompaniment

SCORE + ECD of parts

Written and arranged by Peter Wilson

FABER *ff* MUSIC

With many thanks to Janice Gillard for all her help

© 2009 by Faber Music Ltd
This edition first published in 2009
74–77 Great Russell Street London WC1B 3DA
Music processed by Jeanne Roberts
Cover design by Lydia Merrills-Ashcroft
Printed in England by Caligraving Ltd
All rights reserved

ISBN10: 0-571-52927-5
EAN13: 978-0-571-52927-8

To buy Faber Music publications or to find out about the full range of titles available
please contact your local music retailer or Faber Music sales enquiries:

Faber Music Ltd, Burnt Mill, Elizabeth Way, Harlow CM20 2HX
Tel: +44 (0) 1279 82 89 82   Fax: +44 (0) 1279 82 89 83
sales@fabermusic.com   fabermusic.com

Contents

Put the CD in a computer to download PDFs of all the instrumental parts
and print out as many of each part as is needed:

Violin I

Violin II

Violin III

Viola

Cello

Double Bass

Open-string violin

Open-string viola

Open-string cello

Piano

Put it in a CD player to hear the free audio tracks of the
piano accompaniments – ideal for rehearsals and performances.
Track 1 gives an A for tuning.

James Bond Theme

Monty Norman

© 1962 EMI United Partnership Ltd
EMI United Partnership Ltd (Publishing) and Alfred Publishing Co (Print)
Administered in Europe by Faber Music Ltd

Licensed to Thrill!

Peter Wilson

© 2009 by Faber Music Ltd

Nobody Does it Better

Words by Carole Bayer Sager
Music by Marvin Hamlisch

© 1977 United Artists Music Co Inc and Unart Music Corp
EMI Music Partnership Ltd (Publishing) and Alfred Publishing Co (Print)
Administered in Europe by Faber Music Ltd

ISBN10:   0-571-52925-9
EAN13: 978-0-571-52925-4

ISBN10:   0-571-52926-7
EAN13: 978-0-571-52926-1

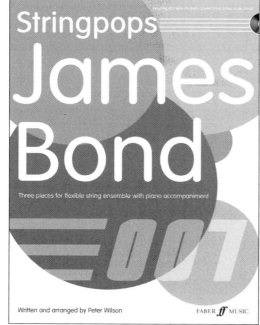

ISBN10:   0-571-52927-5
EAN13: 978-0-571-52927-8

ISBN10:   0-571-52928-3
EAN13: 978-0-571-52928-5

FABER *ff* MUSIC

To buy Faber Music publications or to find out about the full range of titles available
please contact your local music retailer or Faber Music sales enquiries:

Faber Music Ltd, Burnt Mill, Elizabeth Way, Harlow CM20 2HX
Tel: +44 (0) 1279 82 89 82   Fax: +44 (0) 1279 82 89 83
sales@fabermusic.com   fabermusic.com   expressprintmusic.com